$ 35.00

W9-CKB-535

A PHOTOGRAPHER'S JOURNEY

GRAEME OUTERBRIDGE

TRAINS

INDIANAPOLIS MARION CO.

PUBLIC LIBRARY

HARRY N. ABRAMS, INC., PUBLISHERS

For Maria with all her magic

"Strong ties carry this visual train across all lands, time flies with the
    wind, and each adventure is one more station away."

Editor: Eric Himmel

Designer: Dirk Luykx

Library of Congress Cataloging-in-Publication Data

Outerbridge, Graeme, 1950–
    Trains : photographs / by Graeme Outerbridge.
        p.   cm.
    ISBN 0–8109–4481–2 (cloth) / ISBN 0–8109–2945–7 (book club
pbk.)
    1. Railroads Pictorial works.   I. Title.
    TF149.098 2000
    779'.966251—dc21   99–41258

Copyright © 2000 Graeme Outerbridge

Published in 2000 by Harry N. Abrams, Incorporated, New York
All rights reserved. No part of the contents of this book may be
reproduced without the written permission of the publisher

Printed and bound in Japan

 Harry N. Abrams, Inc.
100 Fifth Avenue
New York, N.Y. 10011
www.abramsbooks.com

CONTENTS

THE PHOTOGRAPHS ARE THE JOURNEY

I grew up with only the memory of trains. A little black toy engine whistled around its track on my bedroom floor. My stepfather's basement was filled with an amazing miniature landscape of model trains. It was magical to turn the lights off and stand in the dark holding the transformer switch, following the engine's small headlight as it weaved around the room. The old Bermuda Railway went out of business five years before I was born, but the track bed ran down North Shore by the sparkling turquoise water and past the front of our white house. Following it west brought me to Bailey's Bay, filled with fishing boats of every color. I would stare at the pylons marching like soldiers across the bay and conjure about trains. I never dreamed that I would one day ride so many.

In 1993, after several years of photographing bridges for a book, my thoughts turned to trains. The resulting project was to span five years and forty journeys, on every continent save Antarctica. During an intense period of travel between 1995 and the early autumn of 1997 my assistant Maria Dzygrynuk and I circled the globe three times catching trains. For weeks on end, the huge steel boa constrictors would swallow us up and regurgitate us at one exotic place after another. Some nights at home in Southampton, Bermuda, I dream of those narrow golden-hued corridors as they heave from side to side to the constant clatter of steel meeting steel. The dream is never frightening. I am arriving at another unknown station. People wait patiently on the platform. In their fleeting faces I see dull routine or expectation at reunion or the sadness of departure.

We were set free in the world like gypsies. Each day's plans were hostage to delays that caused late arrivals and missed connections. Detached as we were from our country, our friends and family, a transparent lightness settled on our spirits. Only the strangers we met on our journey prevented us from becoming invisible. Conversations with travelers en route would invariably add more train journeys that were not to be missed. What started out to be a vision of certain train travel ended with a process of not letting structure get in the way of the moment and serendipity. More than any itinerary, speed, time, and place established our coordinates on the surface of the land. Friends in foreign lands helped anchor us, reclaimed us from the lonely breeze of our journey. Stopping to visit, we would develop film, contact travel and train companies, and organize the next leg of our train adventure.

Sometimes during these short pauses I would attempt to figure out a new approach to the photographic subject. There are only so many different ways to photograph a train coming around a curve. I shot from inside engine cabs, leaning out of open windows while careening along at high speed, standing on engine catwalks, and from the roofs of carriages. Everywhere, railway workers took care of me. They kept an eye on me when I took my chances and cautioned me when close to danger. It was a great pleasure to meet them and to be a part of their working day. I was honored to be allowed to join their family.

The interesting pictures always seemed to be where the railroad companies didn't want me to wander. Certain scenes exerted a gravitational pull and I would feel myself drifting heedlessly past barricades posted "danger high voltage" or "keep out." This risk-taking led to a couple of arrests and, in each case, I was happily released without charges being filed.

I'm not the typical train photographer, nor do I have the rail fan's exact metaphysics concerning every detail of railroading. My approach was to treat each train as a new experience and let the journey reveal hidden facets. I wanted to find a visual language to express the experience of train travel. I did my best to capture the sense of movement in my photographs, but of course the sounds of the road and the smell of diesel are missing. A train whistle in the night conjures dreams. One feels an excitement of possibilities; maybe it's the call to adventure or the promise of escape from troubles that feel inescapable. Sound announces a train: unless you're in the desert, you always hear the whistle before the train comes into view. The strong shrill blast of a freight meeting a deadline is the sound of power and industry. At dusty little crossings, red lights dance their warning accompanied by clanging bells.

The journey is over, leaving a scattering of memories. Between Nairobi and Mombassa, a clutch of chickens in the next compartment cluck all night and sleep eludes me. An engineer who has survived a crash into a wheat trailer tells me about it on his first day back at work as we sit up in the engineer's cab rushing through the Australian outback. Way up in the Canadian Shield a lone wolf on a frozen white pond pauses, looks at the train, and then walks on. Silver pools of water on a little station platform in New Zealand reflect a clearing sky. On a clear blue day, the red engine of the Glacier Express threads a snowy Swiss mountain pass. As we back into the station at Killarney, Ireland, the smell of burning peat is everywhere and the emerald green hills are dotted with sheep and cattle. Endless Malaysian rubber plantations. That fine gray-white dust of China and the ruins of the Western Great Wall. The impressions are as varied as the landscapes that the trains traverse.

There were long periods when I became discouraged and lost my way. Sometimes a special vision would appear and I would not raise my camera but let it go free along its momentary path. It was enlightening not to hunt it down but to file it away in my mind. In a blur it would be out of view and gone again, and I would feel refreshed.

The adventure was time well spent in the world of trains and the places they go. The photographs are a record of what captured my attention as the journey unfolded.

Graeme Outerbridge
Southampton, Bermuda
May 1999

TRACKS

Tracks to the highlands, Scotland

Shane's Castle Railway, Antrim, Northern Ireland

Rails, Scotland

Entering Folkestone, England

The El Transcantabrico, Northern Spain

Rails, Thailand

Mount Washington Cog Railway, New Hampshire

The Indian Pacific, Cook, Australia

Switchbacks, Devil's Nose, Ecuador

Grain elevators, Alberta, Canada

View from the cab of the Ghan, near Alice Springs, Australia

Drying jeans on the
Guayaquil & Quito
Railway, Ecuador

Signal tower and train crossing, Athlone, Ireland

Clearing skies, Greymouth Station, New Zealand

STATIONS

Train approaching
Heuston Station,
Dublin

Waiting commuters,
Waverly Station,
Edinburgh

Afternoon station shadows, Spain

Cantt Station, New Delhi

Rathmore
Station, Ireland

The Spirit of the
Outback at
Emerald Station,
Australia

Cork Station,
Ireland

Work crew,
Athenry
Station, Ireland

The Sierra Madre Express at Posanda Barrancas Station, Mexico.

Opposite: The street market quickly dissolves and recreates itself as the steam train passes through Milagro, Ecuador

Mombasa Railway
Station, Kenya

Kuranda Station,
Queensland,
Australia

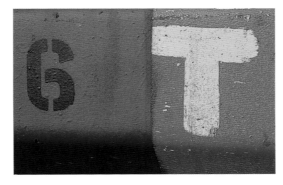

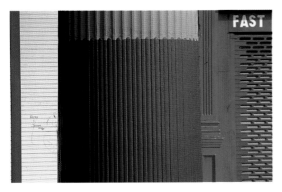
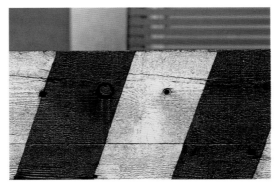

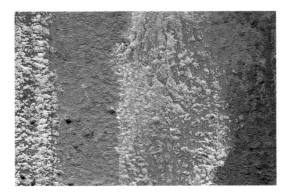
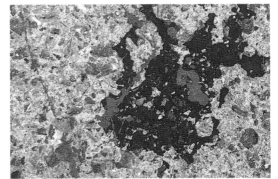

Cuenca Station high up in the Andes, Ecuador

Cantt Station, New Delhi, India

POWER

Full steam
ahead on the
Guayaquil &
Quito Railway,
Ecuador

Inspecting the engine at Glenfinnan Station before crossing the famous concrete viaduct, Scotland

Waiting for an engine, Liuyan Station, China

Loading water on
the Guayaquil &
Quito Railroad,
Ecuador

Crewman,
Guayaquil &
Quito Railway

Signaling to the
engineer,
Divisadero Station,
Mexico

Shunting cars,
St. Moritz Station,
Switzerland

Engineer,
Tashkent,
Uzbekistan

Engine, Kazakhstan

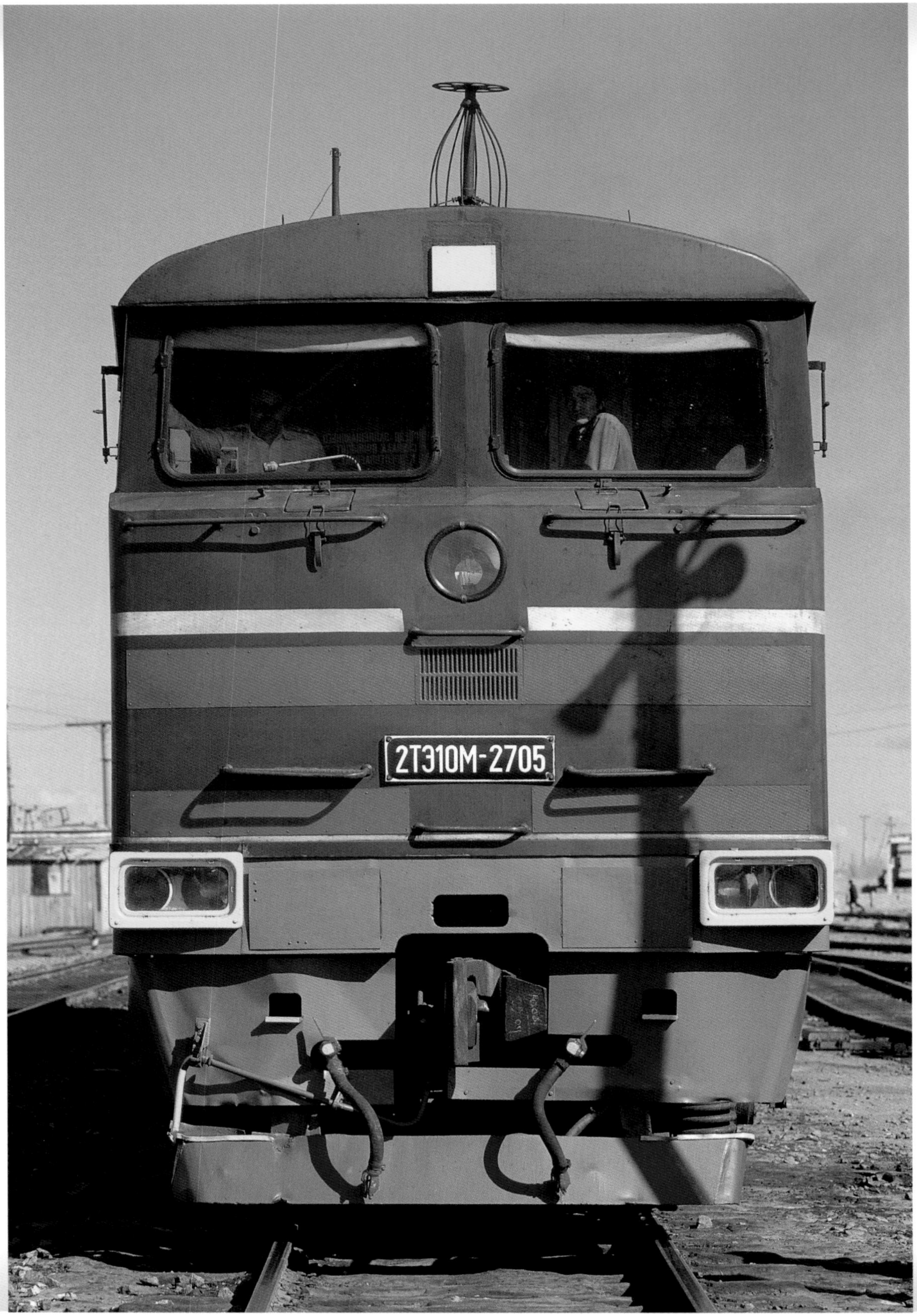

Bringing up a new
engine, Lintong
Station, China

Mount
Washington
Cog Railway,
New
Hampshire

Freight train
near Almaty,
Kazakhstan

Railyard, Jiayuguan Station, with the Qilian Shan mountains in the distance, China

Solitary engine,
Urgench,
Uzbekistan

Freight trains
near Urgench,
Uzbekistan

The Canadian pulls out of Jasper, Canada

Trainyard, St. Moritz Station, Switzerland

Dart commuter train near Connelly Station, Dublin

On the Belfast run, Connolly Station, Dublin

View of the Channel Tunnel construction site from Shakespeare Cliffs, Dover, England

Entering the tunnel, Folkestone, England

Platform canopies, Folkestone

Automobile carriers, tunnel train

Leaving the tunnel, Folkestone

Engine, Romney, Hythe & Dymchurch Railway, England

The Sunlander,
Queensland,
Australia

FEVE
commuter train,
northern Spain

Engine,
Queensland Rail,
Australia

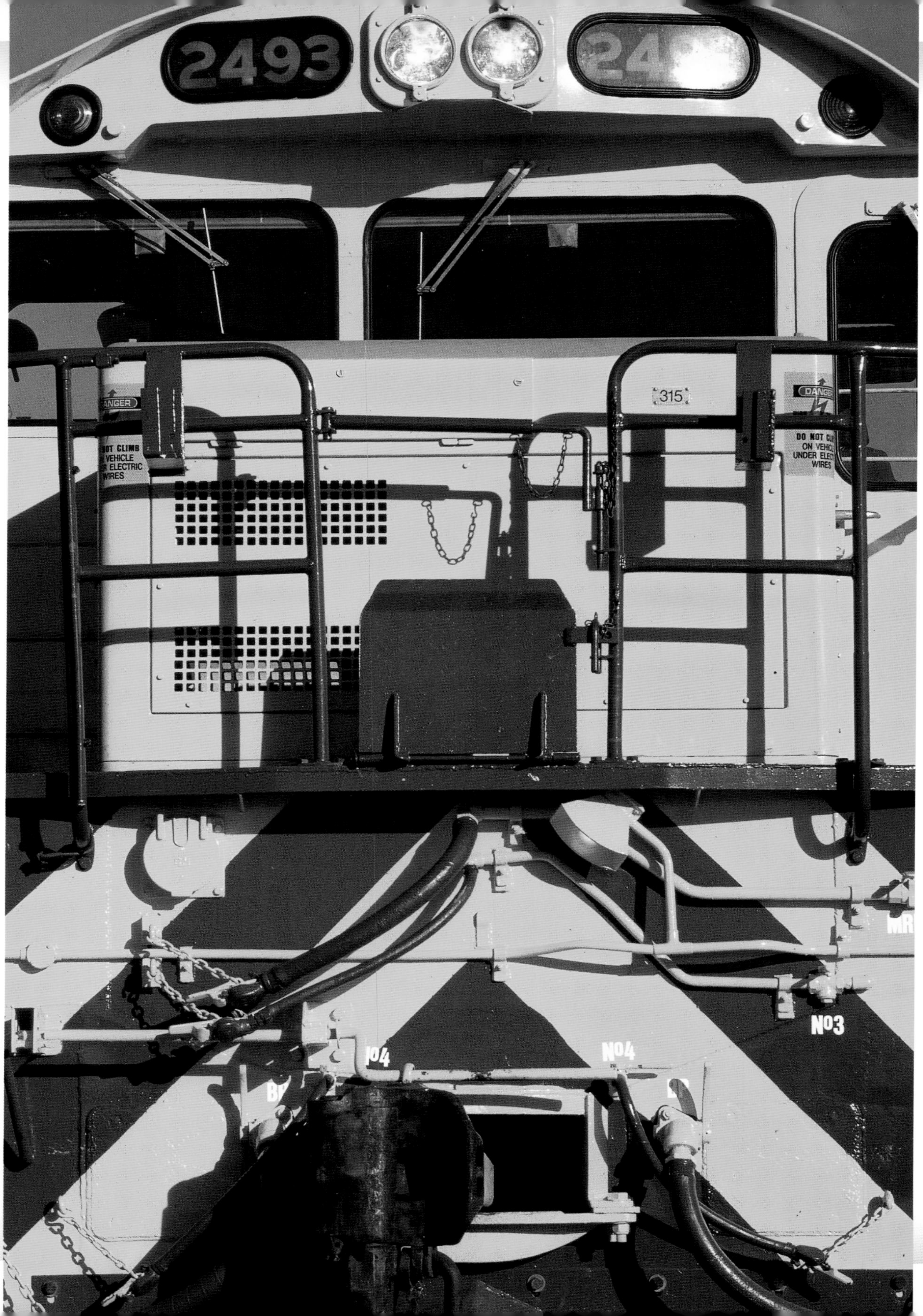

Engine,
Queensland
Rail,
Australia

Engine, Indian
Railways, India

Engine,
FNdeM,
Mexico

Engine, Kenya
Railways,
Kenya

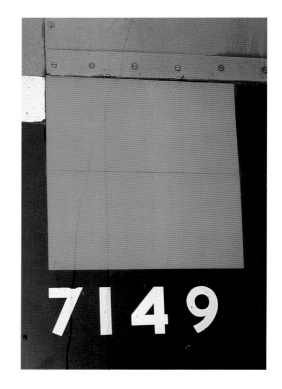
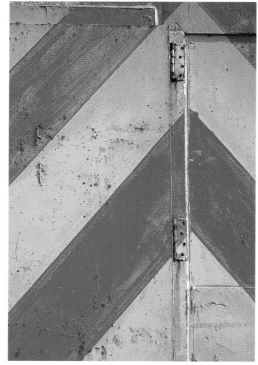

Engine,
Amtrak, United
States

Engine, Sierra
Madre Express,
Mexico

Engine, VIA Rail,
Canada

Caboose, Pacifico
Norte, Mexico

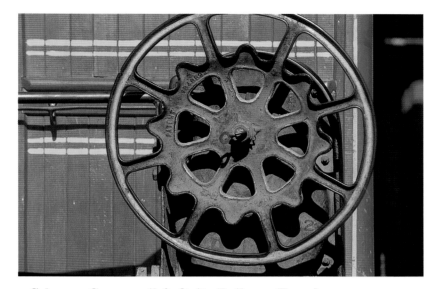

Caboose, Guayaquil & Quito Railway, Ecuador

Caboose, Pacifico Norte, Mexico

Caboose, Sante Fe Southern Railroad, New Mexico

Caboose, FNdeM, Mexico

Morning, Cantt Station, New Delhi

Sundown, Longreach Station,

TRAVEL

Inter-city express crossing the Rio Negro, Luarca, Spain

The Spirit of the
Outback,
Queensland,
Australia

Observation car "Strathcona Park," The Canadian

Observation car "New York," American Orient Express

Observation car "New York"

Carriage roof, The Ghan, Adelaide, Australia

Cabin stewards
stand at their posts,
Beijing Main
Station, China

Cabin steward
greeting returning
passengers, the
Palace on Wheels,
India

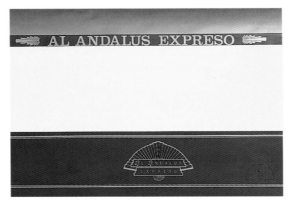

Station master, Asturias, Spain

Porter, Guayaquil & Quito Railway, Ecuador

Train official, Bukhara, Uzbekistan

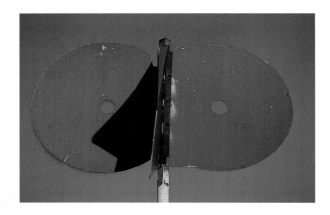
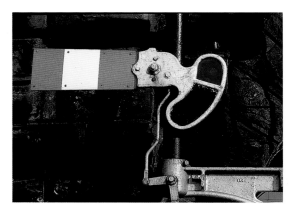
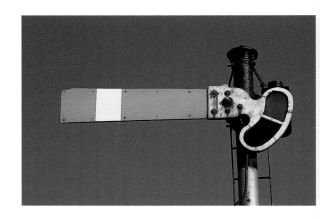
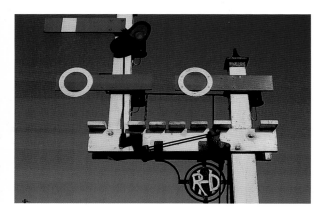
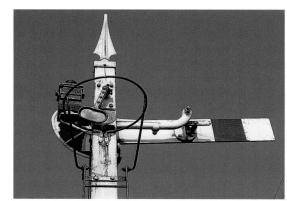
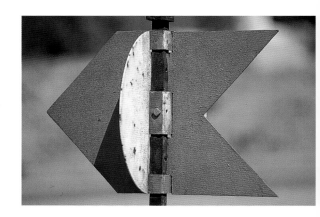

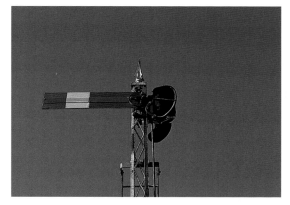
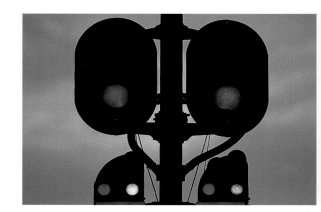

Opposite: Signals near Stoney Creek Falls, Kuranda, Australia

Shadow of the Sierra Madre Express in the bed of the Río Fuerte, Mexico

FROM A MOVING TRAIN

Tracks of the
Canadian

ITINERARY

The following list includes the major routes traveled in the course of this project.

AFRICA

Kenya Railways, traveling between Nairobi and Mombasa.

ASIA

China Orient Express, traveling from Beijing to Alatao (Chinese/Kazak border), via Xi'an, Jiayunguan, Liuyuan, and Turfan.

Eastern & Oriental Express, traveling between Bangkok and Singapore, via Hua Hin, Hatyai, Padang Besar (Thai-Malay border), Butterworth, and Kuala Lumpur.

Nostalgic Istanbul Orient Express, traveling from Alatao (Chinese/Kazak border) to Moscow, via Almaty (Kazakhstan), Tashkent (Uzbekistan), and Urgench.

Palace on Wheels, rail tour originating in Delhi, with stops in Jaipur, Chittaurgarh, Sawai Madhopur, Jaisalmer, Jodhpur, and Bharatpur/Fatehpur Sikri.

AUSTRALIA

Indian Pacific, traveling between Perth and Sydney, Australia, via Kalgoorlie, Cook, Port Augusta, and Adelaide. Trackage through Cook is the longest stretch of straight track in the world (296 miles).

Kuranda Scenic Railway, between Cairns and Kuranda, Australia.

The Ghan, traveling between Adelaide and Alice Springs, Australia.

The Queenslander and Sunlander, between Brisbane and Cairns, Australia.

The Spirit of the Outback, between Brisbane and Longreach, Australia.

The Tranzalpine, traveling between Christchurch and Graymouth, New Zealand, via Arthur's Pass.

EUROPE

Al Andalus Express, rail tour originating in Seville, Spain, and stopping in Córdoba, Granada, and Ronda.

El Transcantabrico, traveling between San Sebastian and Santiago de Compostela, Spain, via Ribadeo, Luarca, Ribadesella, Llanes, Santillana del Mar, and Laredo.

British Rail, inter-city express traveling between London and Edinburgh.

Glacier-Express, traveling between Zermatt and St. Moritz, Switzerland, via Chur, Andermatt, and Brig.

Iarnród Éireann/Irish Rail, routes to Dublin, Rosslare Harbour, Tralee, and Belfast.

Northern Irish Railway, traveling between Belfast and Derry.

Romney, Hythe & Dymchurch Railway, between Hythe and Dungeness, England.

Shane's Castle Railway, between Shane's Castle and Antrim, Ireland.

The Royal Scotsman, rail tour to Edinburgh, Keith, Dingwall, Kyle of Lochalsh, Elgin, Keith, Carrbridge, Spean Bridge, Glenfinnan, Fort William, and Taynuilt, Scotland.

NORTH AMERICA

The Canadian, traveling between Toronto and Vancouver, Canada, via Sudbury, Winnipeg, Saskatoon, Edmonton, Jasper, and Kamloops.

The Great Transcontinental Journey, rail tour traveling between Los Angeles and Washington, D. C., via Santa Fe, San Antonio, Houston, New Orleans, Birmingham, and Charlottesville.

The Mt. Washington Cog Railway, to the summit of Mt. Washington, New Hampshire.

SOUTH AMERICA

Guayaquil & Quito Railway, traveling between Guayaquil and Quito, Ecuador, via Duran, Bucay, Huigra, Sibambe, Alausi, Palmira, Riobamba, Urbina, Mocha, Ambato, and Cotopaxi.

Sierra Madre Express, rail tour of the Copper Canyon, Mexico, traveling from Magdalena to Nogales, via Divisadero.

ACKNOWLEDGMENTS

Roxy Kaufmann, John Kaufmann, Cece Mead, David Mead, Gregory Toleram, Raj Toleram, Dennis Sherwin, Paola Dzygrynuk, Basil Dzygrynuk, Damiana Dzygrynuk, Yeaton Outerbridge, Betsey Outerbridge, Peter Dzygrynuk, Julie Dzygrynuk, Lewis Outerbridge, Marie Foster, Louisa Outerbridge, Elizabeth Outerbridge, Henry Kartagener, Chris Skow, Margaret Wulenga, Pilar Vico, Patricia Rondelli, Vicky Brems, Oliva Burrett, Peggy Bendel, Dennis Hofilena, Gary Cullen, Ted Chin, Libby Wood, Tom Smith, Morag Smith, Gerard Bocquenet, Dominique Bocquenet, Michael Royce, Annette Royce, Will Kempe, Michelle Jeffers, Chris Gibbons, Mark Kaufmann, Susanne Kaufmann, Christopher Menefee, Edward Menefee, Paula Menefee, Henry Togna, Andrew Outerbridge, Phoebe Outerbridge, George Vaughn, Martha Vaughn, Barbara Vaughn, Susan Simmons, Hermano Froias, Douglas Outerbridge, Ruth Ann Outerbridge, Bayard Outerbridge, Benjamin Outerbridge, Gilbert Darrell, Coralita Darrell, Jim Lyndon, Bernie Lynch, Phil Bussell, Andrea Bussell, Alexandra Outerbridge, David Outerbridge, Adam Outerbridge, David Broham, Patrick Dooley, Gerrit Fokkema, Ebsie Gaines, John Hemingway, Basil Haddrell, Debbie Haddrell, Cathy Quealy, Andrew Krueger, Calla Krueger, Roddy Smith, Leslie Smolan, Asish Bahuguna, Kishore Seegoolam, Peggy Bendel, Kate Fiennes-Price, Dianne Graham, Bill Pickeral, Adrian Bartels, Carolyn Stout, Andre McNally, Trish Parsons, Olivia Barrett, Kenry Heldon, Bruce Smith, David Sugden, Peter Njoroge, Philip Adeane, John Hamlen, Ann Slee, Lord O'Neill, Stuart Martin, Nadia Stanioff, James B. Sherwood, Ken Williams, Chris Hudson, Roseclaire Simmons, Katrina Harrison, Valerie Hayward, Carol Ann Daniels, Adrianna Mussenden, Belinda Woolridge, Peter Willis, Don Westmoreland, Christa Brantsch-Harness, Alex Outerbridge, Jason Outerbridge, Jeanne Outerbridge, Herbert Haag, Charles Barclay, David Gibbons, James Gibbons, Maybeth Fenton, Susan McCloud, Scott McCloud, Barry Clark, Dot Clark, Shorty Trimingham, Dot Trimingham, Wendell Hollis, Albert Mussner, Julian Hall, Michael Scott, Michael Misick, Gretchen Misick, John Misick, Stuart Outerbridge, Alex Obolensky, Paul Obolensky, Neil Nanda, Ken Hansen, Mark Epstein, Bill Kempe, Shelia Kempe, Creighton Greene, Jeff Conyers, Edie Conyers, Paget Wharton, Tim Hodgson, Andrew Holbrow, Michelle Jeffers, Don Westmoreland, Dirk Luykx, Eric Himmel, and Paul Gottlieb.

Graeme Outerbridge